A Year to R

1964

For Those Whose Hearts Belong to 1964

Celebrating your year

1964

A memorable year for

....

....

....

....

....

....

....

Contents

Introduction

A Year to Remember - 1964
For Those Whose Hearts Belong to 1964

To our cherished readers who hold a special connection to the year 1964, whether it's because you were born in this remarkable year, celebrated a milestone, or hold dear memories from that time, this book is a tribute to you and your unique connection to an unforgettable era.

In the pages that follow, we invite you to embark on a captivating journey back to 1964, a year of profound historical significance. For those with a personal connection to this year, it holds a treasure trove of memories, stories, and experiences that shaped the world and touched your lives.

Throughout this book, we've woven together the tapestry of 1964, providing historical insights, personal stories, and interactive activities that allow you to relive and celebrate the significance of this special year.

As you turn the pages and immerse yourself in the events and culture of 1964, we hope you'll find moments of nostalgia, inspiration, and the opportunity to rekindle cherished memories of this extraordinary year.

This book is dedicated to you, our readers, who share a unique bond with 1964. May it bring you joy, enlightenment, and a deeper connection to the rich tapestry of history that weaves through your lives.

With warm regards,
Edward Art Lab.

Chapter 1:
Politics and Leading Events around the World

1.1 The Global Stage in 1964: Where Were You?

The year 1964 was a pivotal moment in world history, marked by significant political and cultural events that shaped the course of nations. It was a time of both upheaval and progress, as societies grappled with change and leaders faced momentous decisions. Let's explore some of the key events that unfolded on the global stage in this transformative year.

Civil Rights Act of 1964 (United States):

The Civil Rights Act of 1964 was signed into law by President Lyndon B. Johnson on July 2, 1964. The Civil Rights Act of 1964 made it illegal to discriminate against someone based on their race, religion, sex, national origin, or the colors of their skin. It also made segregation in public places illegal, enforced the desegregation of schools and addressed unfair and unequal access to voting and voter registration.

The law was considered one of the crowning achievements during the civil rights movement and ended the Jim Crow laws that had legalized segregation in the United States since the end of slavery and the Civil War. While it did not solved the country's racial issues or end prejudice, it was the first step in creating a more fair and equal society.

Gulf of Tonkin Incident (Vietnam War):

In early August 1964, two U.S. destroyers stationed in the Gulf of Tonkin in Vietnam radioed that they had been fired upon by North Vietnamese forces. In response to these reported incidents, President Lyndon B. Johnson requested permission from the U.S. Congress to increase the U.S. military presence in Indochina. On August 7, 1964, Congress passed the Gulf of Tonkin Resolution, authorizing President Johnson to take any measures he believed were necessary to retaliate and to promote the maintenance of international peace and security in southeast Asia. This resolution became the legal basis for the Johnson and Nixon Administrations prosecution of the Vietnam War.

The War on Poverty and the Introduction of Medicare in 1964

In 1964, President Lyndon B. Johnson launched a "war on poverty" in the United States. This marked a significant moment in American history as he introduced several federal welfare programs, including Medicare. Medicare was a crucial initiative that provided healthcare coverage for senior citizens, addressing a pressing need for affordable medical care among the elderly. These efforts aimed to reduce poverty, improve education and healthcare access, and promote social equality in the United States, reflecting a major step towards a more inclusive society.

Apartheid in South Africa: In 1964, Nelson Mandela and several other anti-apartheid leaders were sentenced to life in prison during the Rivonia Trial in South Africa. Mandela's imprisonment became a symbol of the struggle against apartheid.

Rio Grande do Sul Uprising (Brazil): In Brazil, a military uprising known as the Rio Grande do Sul Uprising took place in 1964. This event contributed to the establishment of a military dictatorship in the country that lasted for several decades.

Malcolm X's Departure from the Nation of Islam: In March 1964, civil rights leader Malcolm X announced his departure from the Nation of Islam, marking a significant shift in his activism and approach to civil rights and social justice.

Khrushchev's Resignation (Soviet Union):

Nikita Khrushchev, the Premier of the Soviet Union, was forced to resign from his position in October 1964. This leadership change had implications for the Cold War dynamics between the U.S. and the USSR.

1.2 Leaders and Statesmen: Movers and Shakers of '64

In 1964, the world was led by a diverse group of statesmen, each facing unique challenges and opportunities. Here are some of the notable leaders who left their mark on history in '64:

Lyndon B. Johnson (United States): Lyndon B. Johnson assumed the U.S. presidency following the assassination of John F. Kennedy in 1963. In '64, he won a landslide victory in the presidential election, solidifying his position as the 36th President of the United States.

Harold Wilson (United Kingdom): Harold Wilson became the Prime Minister of the United Kingdom in '64, leading the Labour Party to victory in the general election. His tenure was marked by social and economic reforms.

Jawaharlal Nehru (India): Although he passed away in May 1964, Jawaharlal Nehru's legacy as the first Prime Minister of India continued to shape the country's politics and foreign policy.

Fidel Castro (Cuba): Fidel Castro led Cuba as Prime Minister and later as President in 1964, solidifying his role as a prominent figure in the Cold War era.

Activity: Historical Crossword Test Your Knowledge of '64

To test your knowledge of the events and figures of 1964, try solving the historical crossword puzzle in the next section. It's a fun way to engage with the history of this significant year.

ACROSS

1. The Prime Minister of the United Kingdom in 1964 (Last Name).
2. The anti-apartheid leader sentenced to life in prison during the Rivonia Trial.
3. The U.S. President who signed the Civil Rights Act of 1964 (First Name).
4. The Prime Minister of India who passed away in 1964 (Last Name).
5. The country where the Rio Grande do Sul Uprising took place in 1964.
6. The incident in the Gulf of Tonkin that led to increased U.S. involvement in Vietnam.
7. The leader of the Soviet Union who resigned in 1964 (Last Name).
8. The civil rights leader who announced his departure from the Nation of Islam in 1964 (Last Name).

DOWN

1. The law that made it illegal to discriminate based on race, religion, or national origin.
2. President Johnson's initiative to combat poverty and inequality in the U.S.

Chapter 2:
The Iconic Movies, TV Shows, and Awards

2.1 Memorable Films of '64

1964 was the fifth year of the 1960s (1960 is like the **Spanish Inquisition; you shouldn't forget about it**), and it more or less represented the mid-point of the historically dramatic decade. The 1950s were long gone, and the rejuvenated American film industry of the 1970s was still a little while away. But between the epics of the prior decade, and the grittier, more provocative movies of the next one, every year within the 1960s still had plenty of distinct movies to offer.

Dr. Strangelove or: How I Learned to Stop Worrying and Love the Bomb'

A compellingly acted and brilliantly written dark comedy about the end of the world, Dr. Strangelove or: How I Learned to Stop Worrying and Love the Bomb is one of Stanley Kubrick's greatest filmmaking achievements. It expertly balances a strange tone throughout, being a serious look at the terror of atomic weapons and Cold War anxieties while also being extremely funny from start to (almost) finish.

t's well-paced, filled with quotable dialogue, and expertly shot, with the performances also being worthy of praise; particularly George C. Scott and Peter Sellers (the latter of whom skillfully plays three different roles). It's one of the greatest films of all time, and as such, also happens to stand out among other great 1964 movies as the best of its year.

Kwaidan

For as good as Onibaba is, there's one Japanese horror movie from 1964 that's arguably even better. That film is Kwaidan, which runs for three hours and tells four distinct horror/fantasy stories, all revolving around supernatural folktales passed down throughout Japanese history.

It could well be the most consistent horror anthology movie of all time, with no segment of the four feeling weak or skippable compared to the others. Much of this is thanks to the assured direction of the legendary Masaki Kobayashi, as well as the film's talented cast, which includes great actors like Tatsuya Nakadai, Tetsurō Tamba, and Takashi Shimura.

The Umbrellas of Cherbourg

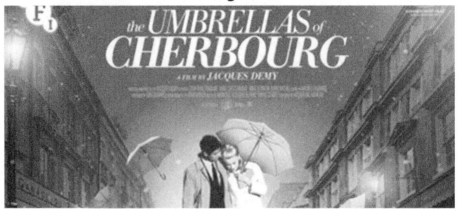

Between Mary Poppins, My Fair Lady, A Hard Day's Night, and now The Umbrellas of Cherbourg, it's safe to say that 1964 was a pretty great year for musicals. This French one's a little more downbeat, as far as music-heavy movies go, being a bittersweet story of young love that's challenged when one of the lovers is shipped off to fight in Algeria.

The Umbrellas of Cherbourg is also notable for being one musical where every single word is sung, rather than spoken, giving it the feeling of a continuous 93-minute-long song. It's an ambitious film where many of its risks pay off, and it's also one that provides plenty to admire visually, thanks to the film's style and use of color.

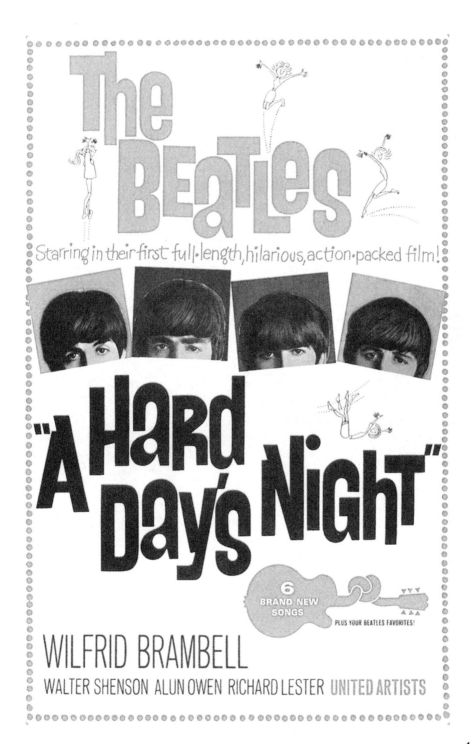

It's not too bold a claim to say that A Hard Day's Night was the best movie The Beatles ever starred in during their short-lived yet impactful time together as a band. In this film, John Lennon, Paul McCartney, George Harrison, and Ringo Starr all play fictionalized versions of themselves, with the film being a loosely plotted "day in the life" style story about the Fab Four getting up to all sorts of mischief in London.

It's a movie that succeeds because of the chemistry between the members of the band (back before the infighting which led to the breakup), the silly humor throughout, and the strength of its songs. The soundtrack album of the same name is often considered the first truly great Beatles album for a reason, foreshadowing greater musical heights that were attained throughout the rest of the 60s.

2.2 TV Shows That Captivated the Nation

Bewitched (1964)

"Bewitched," which enchanted audiences from 1964 to 1972, was a whimsical TV sitcom blending magic, romance, and humor. Set in the 20th century, it followed the charming escapades of a witch, her husband, and their eccentric family in New York and Connecticut.

The Addams Family (1964)

In 1964, "The Addams Family" offered a satirical twist on the American nuclear family, celebrating the macabre and bizarre. This darkly humorous show, rooted in the '60s, delighted viewers with its eccentric characters and spooky abode.

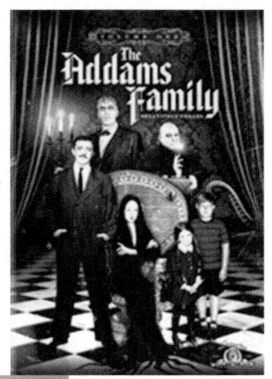

The Munsters (1964)

"The Munsters" (1964) invited viewers into the home of a family of benign monsters. With a mix of sitcom and spooky elements, it playfully blended vampires, Frankensteins, and more in a 1960s setting.

Voyage to the Bottom of the Sea (1964)

"Voyage to the Bottom of the Sea" plunged viewers into underwater adventures, featuring submarines, sea monsters, and time travel. A suspenseful '60s series that explored the depths of the

The Man from U.N.C.L.E. (1964)

In 1964, "The Man from U.N.C.L.E." was the epitome of espionage. Set in New York during the '60s, it followed two secret agents on daring missions, providing a thrilling glimpse into the Cold War era.

Jonny Quest (1964)

"Jonny Quest" (1964) followed the adventures of a boy and his scientist father. With a blend of animation, retro style, and mystery, it offered thrilling escapades in a futuristic '60s setting.

Daniel Boone (1964)

"Daniel Boone" (1964) took viewers to the American frontier in the 18th century. This action-adventure series, set in Kentucky, explored encounters with Native Americans and colonialism.

Gomer Pyle: USMC (1964)

"Gomer Pyle: U.S.M.C." (1964) brought humor to military life in California. This sitcom followed the misadventures of a lovable Marine, reminding us of the lighter side of discipline in the '60s.

Gomer Pyle: USMC (1964)

Let's summarize the 36th Academy Awards in 1964

Date: April 13, 1964
Venue: Santa Monica Civic Auditorium
Honoring Films Released in 1963
Highlights: Winners & Nominees

Cinematography: James Wong Howe and Leon Shamroy won for "Hud" and "Cleopatra."

Directing: Tony Richardson won the Oscar for directing "Tom Jones."

Memorable Moments

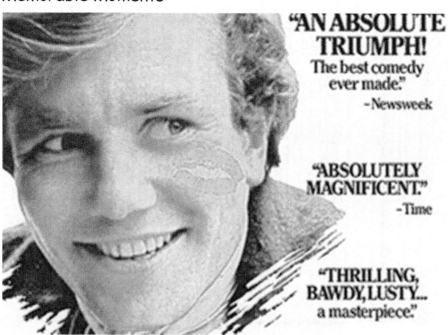

"AN ABSOLUTE TRIUMPH! The best comedy ever made."
-Newsweek

"ABSOLUTELY MAGNIFICENT."
-Time

"THRILLING, BAWDY, LUSTY... a masterpiece."

Sidney Poitier won **Best Actor** for "Lilies of the Field," presented by Anne Bancroft.

Actor in a Supporting Role: Melvyn Douglas (Winner - "Hud")

Actress: Patricia Neal (Winner - "Hud")

Actress in a Supporting Role: Margaret Rutherford (Winner - "The V.I.P.s")

Activity: Movie and TV Show Trivia Quiz – How Well Do You Know '64 Entertainment?

Instructions: Test your knowledge of the iconic movies, TV shows, and awards from the year 1964. Circle the correct answer for each question. Good luck!

1. Which Stanley Kubrick film from 1964 is known for its dark comedy about the Cold War and nuclear weapons?

a) 2001: A Space Odyssey

b) A Clockwork Orange

c) Dr. Strangelove or: How I Learned to Stop Worrying and Love the Bomb

d) Spartacus

2. Which Japanese horror movie from 1964 features four distinct supernatural stories?

a) Onibaba

b) Godzilla vs. Mothra

c) Kwaidan

d) Rashomon

3. What's unique about "The Umbrellas of Cherbourg," a 1964 French musical?

a) It's a downbeat war movie.

b) Every word in the film is sung.

c) It's a documentary about umbrellas.

d) It features famous Hollywood actors.

4. Which 1964 film stars The Beatles and portrays a day in their lives in London?

a) Yellow Submarine

b) Help!

c) A Hard Day's Night

d) Magical Mystery Tour

5. What was the name of the TV sitcom that featured a witch, her husband, and their eccentric family, and ran from 1964 to 1972?
a) The Addams Family
b) The Munsters
c) Bewitched
d) I Dream of Jeannie

6. In 1964, which TV series was known for its espionage adventures during the Cold War era?
a) The Twilight Zone
b) The Man from U.N.C.L.E.
c) Mission: Impossible
d) The X-Files

7. Who won the Oscar for Best Actor in 1964 for the film "Lilies of the Field"?
a) Albert Finney
b) Sidney Poitier
c) Richard Harris
d) Paul Newman

7. Who won the Oscar for Best Actor in 1964 for the film "Lilies of the Field"?
a) Albert Finney
b) Sidney Poitier

c) Tom Jones
d) Kwaidan

9. Which film from 1964 is famous for having every single word in the movie sung, rather than spoken?
a) The Sound of Music
b) Mary Poppins
c) West Side Story
d) The Umbrellas of Cherbourg

10. Who won the Oscar for Best Actress in 1964 for her role in "Hud"?
a) Shirley MacLaine
b) Rachel Roberts
c) Patricia Neal
d) Leslie Caron

Scoring:
0-3 Correct: Novice in 1964 Pop Culture
4-6 Correct: A Fan of the Classics
7-9 Correct: 1964 Pop Culture Enthusiast
10 Correct: 1964 Pop

Let's color and give it to yourself!

33

Chapter 3:
Top Songs, Albums, and Awards

3.1 Renowned Musicians and Bands of '64

In the vibrant musical landscape of 1964, several legendary musicians and bands made their mark, contributing to the rich tapestry of the era's music. Let's journey back and explore the iconic artists who defined this remarkable year.

The Beatles

In 1964, The Beatles experienced an unprecedented level of success and cultural impact that is often referred to as "Beatlemania." Here are some key details about The Beatles in 1964:

Album Releases: In 1964, The Beatles released two critically acclaimed albums in the United States. "Meet the Beatles!" and "The Beatles' Second Album" both topped the Billboard charts, solidifying their status as musical superstars

International Tours: The band embarked on a series of international tours in 1964, including a historic tour of North America. Their concerts were met with fervent fan hysteria, with screaming crowds of young fans often drowning out the music.

Continued Success: The Beatles' success in 1964 was just the beginning of their legendary career. They continued to release groundbreaking albums and singles throughout the 1960s, solidifying their status as one of the greatest bands in the history of popular music.

The
BEATLES
★ IN THEIR 1st U. S. CONCERT PERFORMANCE ★

· FEATURING ·

The
Caravelles

♪

Tommy Roe

♪

The
Chiffons

WASHINGTON SPORTS ARENA
WASHINGTON, D. C.

FEB. 11th - 1964
ALL TICKETS $5.00 (26)

3.2 Notable Song Releases

1964's Top 10 Hot Pop Songs & Music Hits

In the dynamic world of 1960s music, the year 1964 stands out as a pivotal moment. It was a year filled with iconic pop songs and music hits that continue to resonate today. Join us as we revisit the top 10 songs that shaped the sound and spirit of this unforgettable year.

1. Chapel Of Love – Dixie Cups

#1 for 3 weeks in 1964, this is probably the best-known Wedding Song of the early rock era.

2. Under The Boardwalk – The Drifters

Lead singer Rudy Lewis died the night before the recording session, and Johnny Moore did the lead vocal for this, written by Artie Resnick and Kenny Young.

3. I Saw Her Standing There – Beatles

This was the B-SIDE for 'I Want To Hold Your Hand' becoming more popular over time than the A-SIDE, and it reached #14 on the Pop Charts.

4. I'm Into Something Good – Herman's Hermits

Released in late 1964, this song helped kickstart The British Invasion, and has been used in several films and television shows over the past few decades. The band name was actually derived from cartoon character Sherman, Mr. Peabody's friend.

5. L.O.V.E. – Nat "King" Cole

This was one Nat's final releases before his death on February 15, 1965, but he did score a Top 20 hit with a remastered duet of 'Unforgettable' with his daughter Natalie in 1991.

6. I Get Around - Beach Boys

The First #1 Hit for the Boys: Brian, Dennis and Carl Wilson, Mike Love and Al Jardine.

7. Rag Doll - The Four Seasons

Although the 4 Seasons maintained a Top Ten presence through 1967, this was their last #1 song until 1975/6's 'December, 1963 (Oh What A Night)'.

8. My Guy - Mary Wells

Mary was the first Motown Star, and this was her first (and only) #1 Hit. She also had an album of Beatles' hits.

9. Fun, Fun, Fun – Beach Boys

The band had members join/quit and rejoin over the years, including: Bruce Johnston, Glen Campbell , David Marks, Ricky Fataar and Blondie Chaplin.

10. I Want To Hold Your Hand – The Beatles

The Beatle's first #1 Hit, and the Biggest Hit of the Year, released January 18, 1964.

3.3 Music Awards and Honors

The 6th Grammy Award ceremony was held on May 12, 1964, at Beverly Hilton in Los Angeles. NARAS honored the artists for their outstanding performance for the year 1963.

1. Grammy Award for Best Female Pop Vocal Performance:

Winner: Barbra Streisand for "People"

Barbra Streisand's rendition of "People" showcased her remarkable vocal talent and contributed to her status as a prominent figure in pop music.

2. Grammy Award for Best Male Country Vocal Performance:

Winner: Roger Miller for "Dang Me"

Roger Miller's performance of "Dang Me" in the country genre highlighted his unique style and humor in his music.

3. Grammy Award for Best Male Pop Vocal Performance:

Winner: Louis Armstrong for "Hello, Dolly!"

Louis Armstrong's iconic recording of "Hello, Dolly!" solidified his legendary status in jazz and popular music.

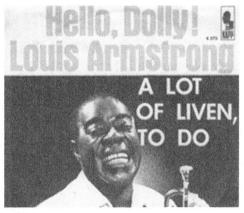

4. Grammy Award for Best Instrumental Soloist Performance (without orchestra):

Winner: Vladimir Horowitz for "Vladimir Horowitz Plays Beethoven, Debussy, Chopin"

Vladimir Horowitz's piano performance showcased his virtuosity and mastery of classical compositions.

5. Grammy Award for Best Instrumental Composition:

Winner: Henry Mancini for "The Pink Panther Theme"

"The Pink Panther Theme" composed by Henry Mancini became an iconic piece of music known for its jazzy and playful melody.

6. Grammy Award for Best Performance by a Vocal Group:

Winner: The Beatles for "A Hard Day's Night"

"A Hard Day's Night" by The Beatles highlighted their har monious vocals and marked their presence in the world of music.

7. Grammy Award for Record of the Year:
Winner: Astrud Gilberto and Stan Getz for "The Girl From Ipanema"
 "The Girl From Ipanema" is a classic bossa nova song that featured Astrud Gilberto and Stan Getz, showcasing their collaboration and musical excellence.

Activity: Music Lyrics Challenge - Guess the Song Lyrics from '64

Instructions: Fill in the missing words in the lyrics of these popular songs from 1964. Test your knowledge of classic songs!

Can you complete the lyrics from the classic song "I Want to Hold Your Hand" by The Beatles, which was a chart-topping hit in 1964? Fill in the blanks to complete the lyrics:

Verse 1:

Oh, yeah, I'll tell you something

I think you'll understand

When I say that something

I want to hold your

_____

I want to hold your

_____

I want to hold your

_____

Chorus:

Oh, please, say to me

You'll let me be your

_____

And please, say to me

You'll let me hold your

_____

Now let me hold your

_____

I want to hold your_____

Verse 2:

And when I touch you, I feel happy

Inside

It's such a feeling that my love

I can't _____

I can't _____

Chorus:

Oh, please, say to me

You'll let me be your

_____

And please, say to me

You'll let me hold your

_____

Now let me hold your

_____

I want to hold your____

Let's color and give it to yourself

OFFICIAL COLORING BOOK

THE
BEATLES

Chapter 4: Sports in 1964

Sports in 1964 were marked by significant events, including the Summer Olympics and notable achievements in various sports. Here are some highlights:

Summer Olympics in Tokyo: The 1964 Summer Olympics were held in Tokyo, Japan. These games were historic as they marked the first time the Olympics were held in Asia. The event showcased various sports, including athletics, swimming, gymnastics, and wrestling. American swimmer Don Schollander and Soviet gymnast Larisa Latynina were among the standout athletes.

Cassius Clay (Muhammad Ali) Becomes World Champion: On February 25, 1964, Cassius Clay (later known as Muhammad Ali) defeated Sonny Liston in a major upset to become the World Heavyweight Champion. Clay famously declared, "I am the greatest," after the fight.

Winter Olympics in Innsbruck: In 1964, the Winter Olympics were held in Innsbruck, Austria. Athletes competed in sports like skiing, ice hockey, figure skating, and bobsleigh. Notable performances included the Soviet Union's domination of ice hockey.

Baseball: In the world of baseball, the St. Louis Cardinals emerged as the World Series champions in 1964, defeating the New York Yankees in a thrilling seven-game series.

Golf: Golfer Arnold Palmer had a successful year in 1964, winning The Masters Tournament and the British Open.

Auto Racing: American driver A.J. Foyt won the prestigious Indianapolis 500 race in 1964.

Track and Field: American sprinter Bob Hayes won two gold medals at the 1964 Olympics, setting records in the 100 meters and the 4x100 meters relay.

Tennis: Australian tennis player Roy Emerson dominated the Grand Slam tournaments in 1964, winning both the Australian Open and the French Open.

Formula One: John Surtees became the Formula One World Champion in 1964, driving for Ferrari.

Activity:
Sports Trivia - Test Your Knowledge of 1964 Sports History

Let's put your knowledge of sports history in 1964 to the test! Below are some trivia questions related to the significant sporting events and achievements of that year. See how many you can answer correctly.

1. Who won the gold medal in the 100 meters at the 1964 Summer Olympics and set a world record in the process?
a) Don Schollander
b) Bob Hayes
c) Larisa Latynina
d) Cassius Clay

2. Which American boxer famously declared, "I am the greatest," after defeating Sonny Liston in 1964 to become the World Heavyweight Champion?
a) Joe Frazier
b) Sugar Ray Robinson
c) Muhammad Ali (Cassius Clay)
d) George Foreman

3. In which city were the 1964 Winter Olympics held?
a) Tokyo, Japan
b) Innsbruck, Austria
c) Rome, Italy
d) Moscow, Russia

4. Which baseball team won the 1964 World Series, defeating the New York Yankees?
a) New York Yankees
b) Los Angeles Dodgers
c) St. Louis Cardinals
d) Boston Red Sox

5. Who was the golfer that achieved success in 1964 by winning both The Masters Tournament and the British Open?
a) Arnold Palmer
b) Jack Nicklaus
c) Gary Player
d) Ben Hogan

6. Which American driver won the prestigious Indianapolis 500 race in 1964?
a) Mario Andretti
b) A.J. Foyt
c) Dale Earnhardt
d) Richard Petty

7. What sport did Australian player Roy Emerson excel in, winning multiple Grand Slam tournaments in 1964?
a) Tennis
b) Golf
c) Cricket
d) Rugby

8. Who became the Formula One World Champion in 1964, driving for Ferrari?
a) Jim Clark
b) Graham Hill
c) John Surtees
d) Jackie Stewart

Chapter 5:
Fashion Popular Leisure Activities

5.1 Fashion Flashback in '64
Vintage 1964 Fashion including Blazers, Dresses, Coats, Shirts and Three Piece Outfits

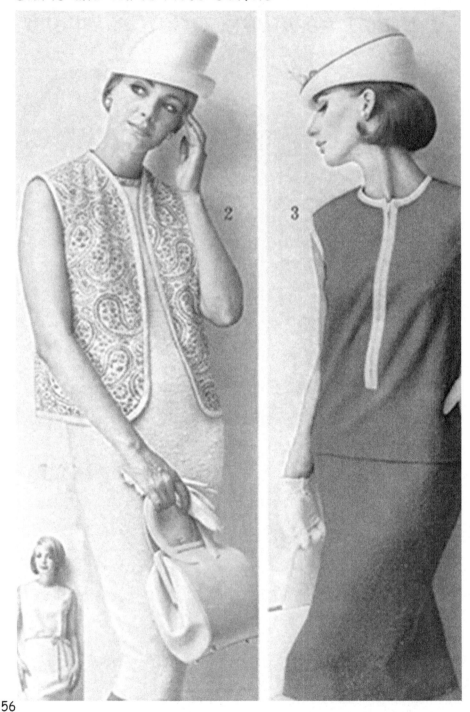

Fashion Clothing From the year 1964 including prices, descriptions and pictures for Ladies and Gentlemens outfits, shirts, dresses etc. The prices shown for these Ladies Clothing Accessories are the price they were sold for in 1964 not today

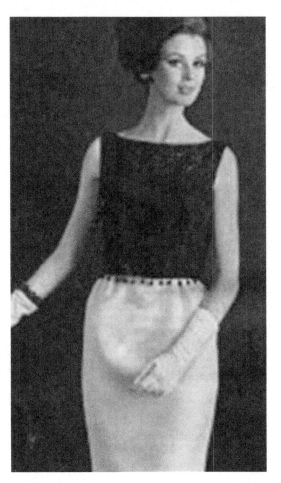

Black and White Over-blouse Dress
Price: $12.54
Description Black and white are paired strikingly in this one-piece dress with an "over-blouse" effect. The Spanish influence is delightfully evident in the black cotton lace top with its ball-fringe trim. White skirt of lustrous rayon and silk. Dress is fully lined. Long back zipper.

Bow Trim Dress
Price: $8.00
Description Bow-trimmed over-blouse dress. Button-back top. Side-zippered skirt. Color combinations to choose from include jade green, cherry red, olive green, lavender and beige print or medium and dark blue, lavender and jade green print.

Cardigan Blazer
Price: $18.50
Description Cardigan rayon blazers. Rakish collarless style. Rayon ascot matches the lining. Colors are Dante red with a figured ascot or indigo blue with a polka-dot ascot.

Collared Dress
Price: $8.00
Description Sweetly collared step-in dress with an all-around cluster-pleated skirt. Choose a print in jade green, cherry red, olive green, lavender and beige or medium and dark blue, lavender and jade green.

.

Front Pleat Dress
Price: $5.00
Description Front-pleat dress has a scoop neck and shirred skirt. Has long back zipper and acetate satin trim with a belt.

Gala Separates
Price: $7.90

Description Gala set, cream-beige separates in cotton and rayon brocade. Double-breasted jacket with three-quarter length sleeves and gold-color buttons. Capri pants with back zipper

Indispensable Dress
Price: $10.00

Description Orlon acrylic and wool jersey in superior seven ounce weight. Carefully lined with acetate taffeta. Dress has self piping at the neckline; triangular stitching above the inverted back kick pleat; skillfully seamed and dart-detailed construction; three inch taped hem; and a non-snag nylon Zephyr zipper in the back. Colors are white, royal blue, black or red.

Lambs Wool and Suede Sweater
Price: $16.86
Description Striking is the word for this rich combination of a lamb's wool body with a V-striped front panel of genuine suede leather. Choose from olive combination or tan combination

Low Waisted Dress
Price: $12.84
Description Low-waisted dress of loopy wool. The deftly seamed bodice is raglan-sleeved, has a modified sailor collar. Skirt is lightly eased. Has a back zipper closing. Colors are medium pink or medium blue.

Men's Shirt Jac
Price: $5.77
Description Shirt-Jacs... casual comfort in a gentlemanly manner. Tapered and tailored to be worn outside like a jacket. Button tabs at wrist adjust for individual fit. Comes in lustrous solid colors and is made with sharkskin fabric. Comes in olive, gray or blue.

61

Oxford Weave Sport Coat
Price: $22.50
Description Warm, earthy mixture of tan into clay, brown and smatterings of blue is accentuated by the classic oxford weave. Made with fifty-five percent Orlon acrylic blended with forty-five percent wool to give the fabric a rugged look, yet it is extremely soft to the hand. Has tailored shoulders and a center vent.

Oxford Weave Sport Coat
Price: $22.50
Description Warm, earthy mixture of tan into clay, brown and smatterings of blue is accentuated by the classic oxford weave. Made with fifty-five per-cent Orlon acrylic blended with forty-five percent wool to give the fabric a rugged look, yet it is ex-tremely soft to the hand. Has tailored shoulders and a center vent.

Ruffled Shirt
Price: $2.97
Description Supima combed cotton broadcloth shirt. Has a Mandarin neck and roll sleeves. Comes in white or medium blue.

In Dress
Price: $12.84
Description Step-in dress with a skirt-in-motion of close-set pleats. Made with acetate and rayon crepe. "Frog" buttons to waist. Self rope belt. Colors are oyster white or black.

Three Piece Suit Dress
Price: $12.84
Description Three-piece suit-dress is made with brocaded cotton and acetate jacket and side-zippered skirt. Sleeveless white acetate crepe blouse buttons in the back. Comes in black on silver gray or medium green on silver gray.

Tie Collar Dress

Price: $5.00

Description Step-In dress with a smart tie-collar. Buttons to waist and has unpressed pleats. Self belt. Color combinations include light blue, deep blue, white and dark green or light olive green, dark olive green, white and peacock blue.

Velvet Dress

Price: $17.84

Description Lovely dress of cotton velveteen. Roll collar dips to a slight v-shape in the back, long sleeves are slit. Has a non-snag nylon Zephyr back zipper closing. Colors to choose from include deep rose pink or copen blue.

Vertical Stripe Shirt Jac

Price: $5.77

Description Vertical accent stripes set on luxurious shirt front of ninety-two percent combed cotton and eight percent silk. The rest of the shirt is one-hundred percent textured rayon. Colors are black with red stripes or black with blue stripes.

5.2 Popular toys

Childhood Toys From The Year 1964 including Rock 'Em Sock 'Em Robots, Tiny Tears Doll, G.I. Joe Figures, Lionel Racing Track and more with prices and descriptions Featured Toys on this page Tiny Tears Doll, G.I. Joe Figures, Lionel Speedway Racing Track, Game Of Mousetrap, Game Of Scrabble, Spinning Tops, Barbies and many more from the 1960sThe prices shown for these Toys are the price they were sold for in 1964 not today

The Beatles Dolls
Price: $1.66 Each
Description The Beatles Dolls including John, Paul, George and Ringo, As Beatlemania and pop music targeted a younger audience 1960s Toys reflected the trend with dolls, Record Players and more.

Musical TV Phonograph

Manufacturer: Playskool

Price: $3.99

Description Listen to the music-box sound of "Skip to my Lou" and watch the children dancing happily on the revolving screen in bright colors. Comes with three records in storage slot.

Hansel and Gretel Models

Price: $5.99 Each

Description Hansel and Gretel Models made by top craftsman in Germany.

Ideal Printing Press

Manufacturer: Price: $11.44

Description Create Your Own Printing Shop to make posters, Ideal Printing Press comes with 2 sets of Type, Ink, Tweezers, Printing Plates and much more.

Jaguar XK-E Model

Price: $7.44

Description Authentic 21 inch Jaguar XK-E Model with 200 pieces, steers, hood goes up and down, doors open, replica 6 cylinder XK-E Engine, wire spoke wheels, working suspension.

200-piece kit

Lionel Speedway Racing Track

Price: $19.88

Description Lionel Speedway Racing Track, includes loop-the-loop, cars race at scale speeds of over 400 MPH and go up and over the loop.

for the most thrilling
HO racing ever

Magilla Gorilla

Price: From $1.88

Description Magilla Gorilla and his TV pals including Punkin Puss, Mushmouse, Droop A Long Coyote, Richochette Rabbit and Magilla Gorilla.

G.I. Joe Figures

Price: $2.32 each

Description Choose from Action Soldier, Action Marine, Action Sailor, or Action Pilot. Each is movable and comes dressed in their respective uniforms.

Scooba Doo Doll

Manufacturer: Mattel

Price: $8.97

Description She's the singing swinger doll, just pull her chatty ring and she says far-out things like "Play it cool... don't be a square." She's 23 inches tall with a soft, cotton-stuffed body and sculpted vinyl head.

Rock 'Em Sock 'Em Robots

Price: $7.99

Description Boxing robots are hand controlled for hours of fun. Boxers move around, throw left and right punches. When socked on the chin, a spring mechanism pops the head up

.

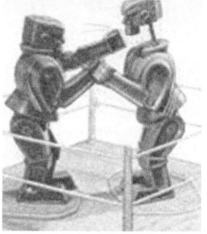

Velveteen Dolls

Price: From $4.98

Description Choose from 9 Velveteen Dolls dressed daintily in the ruffles and colors little girls love.

.

Game Of Mousetrap

Manufacturer: Ideal
Price: $3.99
Description Catch the mouse with the wildest trap ever in the Game Of Mousetrap.

mouse trap game
by Ideal
Catch "mice" with wildest trap ever
$3⁹⁹
www.thepeoplehistory.com

Old Women In A Shoe

Manufacturer: Fisher Price
Price: $3.59
Description Old Women In A Shoe Plays Nursery Rhyme while windows open and close and the toe raises to show more children.

$3⁵⁹

Petite Princess Furniture

Manufacturer: Ideal
Price: From 99 cents
Description The most luxurious Furniture ever offered perfect in every detail Petite Princess Furniture choices include Grand Piano, Living Room, Bedroom, Royal Dressing Table and much more.

70

Activity:
Fashion Design Coloring Page - Create Your '64-Inspired Outfit

Share your 1964 photos,

Don't forget to show off your fabulous '60s fashion

Chapter 6:
Technological Advancements
and Popular Cars

6.1 Technology

Introduction of BASIC Programming Language (1964)
In the year 1964, the world of computer programming saw a significant milestone with the introduction of BASIC (Beginners' All-purpose Symbolic Instruction Code). This high-level programming language was designed with simplicity in mind, making it accessible and easy to learn for beginners and aspiring programmers. BASIC would go on to play a pivotal role in the democratization of computer programming, empowering individuals to write their own software and contributing to the growth of the computing industry.

IBM's Announcement of the System/360 (1964)

1964 marked a transformative moment in the world of computing when IBM made a groundbreaking announcement—the System/360. This innovative computer system represented a major leap forward in terms of compatibility and scalability. It offered a unified platform that could cater to a wide range of computing needs, from small businesses to large enterprises. IBM's System/360 laid the foundation for modern computer architecture and became a cornerstone of the computing industry.

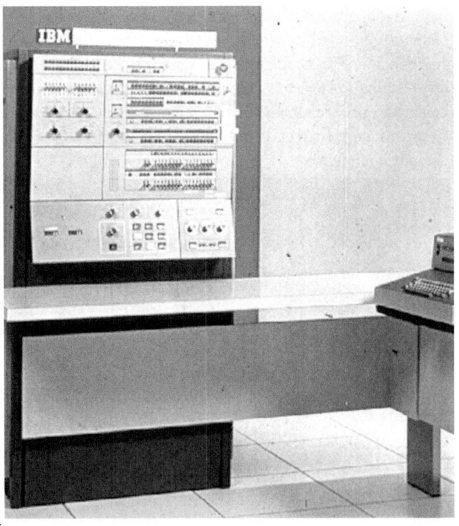

Inauguration of the World's First High-Speed Rail Network in Japan (1964)

Japan rewrote the history of transportation in 1964 by inaugurating the world's first high-speed rail network. This remarkable achievement revolutionized train travel, setting new standards for speed and efficiency. The introduction of high-speed trains not only transformed Japan's domestic transportation but also served as a model for similar developments worldwide, ushering in a new era of rapid rail travel.

Manufacture of the First Ford Mustang (1964)

1964 witnessed the birth of an automotive legend—the Ford Mustang. This iconic American muscle car made its debut and captured the hearts of car enthusiasts worldwide. With its sleek design, powerful performance, and affordability, the Ford Mustang became an instant classic. It symbolized the spirit of the 1960s and remains an enduring symbol of American automotive innovation.

Sony's Introduction of the First VCR Home Video Recorder (1964)

The year 1964 marked a significant moment in the history of home entertainment with Sony's introduction of the first VCR (Video Cassette Recorder) Home Video Recorder. This groundbreaking technology allowed people to record and playback television programs, giving rise to the concept of time-shifting and changing how audiences

Debut of the First Driverless Train on the London Underground (1964)

In 1964, the London Underground made history by launching the world's first driverless train. This technological marvel showcased automation in public transportation and marked a significant step toward efficient and safe mass transit systems. The driverless train set a precedent for the future of automated transportation and urban mobility.

China's First Nuclear Bomb Explosion (1964)

The year 1964 witnessed a significant development in global geopolitics as China conducted its first successful nuclear bomb explosion. This event marked China's entry into the group of nations possessing nuclear capabilities, reshaping the dynamics of the Cold War era. China's nuclear test had far-reaching implications for international relations and security.

Notable Inventions and Inventors (1964)

Several notable inventions emerged in 1964, each making a unique contribution to technology and daily life:
Computer Mouse (USA) by Douglas Engelbart: Douglas Engelbart introduced the computer mouse, a revolutionary input device that transformed how users interacted with computers. This invention laid the foundation for modern computer interfaces and navigation.

6.2 The Automobiles of '64

Best Cars Of 1964 – The Greatest Cars In The World This Year

The US Auto industry was hampered by strikes and parts shortages in 1964 but finished the calendar year with near-record production and sales figures. According to final, unofficial tabulations by Automotive News, 7,746,000 passenger cars rolled off the lines.

1964 Porsche 911

In the year 1963, Porsche unveiled a groundbreaking model at the Frankfurt Motor Show, known as the Porsche 911. This introduction was part of Porsche's strategic move to complement their existing Porsche 356C with a larger 6-cylinder engine. The Porsche 911 would go on to become an iconic sports car, leaving an indelible mark on automotive history. To learn more about this legendary vehicle, delve into its fascinating history and evolution.

1964 Aston Martin DB5 Vantage

September 1964 witnessed the revelation of a remarkable automobile, the DB5 Vantage prototype known as DP217, by Aston Martin. What set this prototype apart was its inclusion of triple Weber twin-choke, sidedraft carburetors and a 5-speed transmission. Aston Martin proudly declared a peak power output of 325 bhp at 5,750 rpm, a notable 40 bhp more than the standard-specification DB5. Discover the exquisite details and engineering that made the DB5 Vantage a standout in the world of luxury sports cars.

1964 Chevrolet Chevelle SS454

In the realm of American muscle cars, the year 1964 brought forth a formidable contender: the Chevrolet Chevelle SS454. At the heart of this powerhouse was the LS6 engine, which was officially rated at 450hp. However, speculation suggests that the LS6 was significantly underrated and may have produced well over 500hp. Explore the muscle and performance of the Chevrolet Chevelle SS454, an icon of the era's automotive muscle.

1964 Lotus Cortina

The collaboration between Ford and Lotus in the early 1960s resulted in the birth of a remarkable sports saloon, the Lotus Cortina. Produced in the United Kingdom from 1963 to 1970, this vehicle was designed as a homologation special to compete in touring car events, Trans-Am racing, and stage rallies. Its compact size, high-powered engine, and racing pedigree made it a force to be reckoned with on the track. Dive into the story of the Lotus Cortina and its impact on motorsport.

1964 Ferrari 500 Superfast

The year 1964 witnessed the debut of a grand tourer that defined luxury and performance—the Ferrari 500 Superfast. Building upon the legacy of the 400 and 410 Super America series, this flagship model offered a grand touring experience with a spacious cabin and a potent V12 engine. With a price tag twice that of the sportier 275 GTB, the 500 Superfast was a rare and exclusive gem, produced in limited quantities. Explore the opulence and power of the Ferrari 500 Superfast.

1964 Pontiac LeMans GTO

1964 marked the birth of an American legend, the Pontiac LeMans GTO. Introduced as a performance option for the Tempest in various body styles, including convertible, coupe, and hardtop, the GTO made an immediate impact. Equipped with a 389 V8 engine producing over 325 hp, this muscle car came with features like a four-barrel carburetor, dual exhaust, and premium tires as standard. Optional enhancements included a 4-speed automatic or manual gearbox, limited slip differential, tachometer, seat belts, power steering, and power brakes. Delve into the history and specifications of the iconic Pontiac LeMans GTO.

Chapter 7: The Cost of Things

7.1 The cost of Living in 1964

The year 1964 marked a distinct era in terms of the cost of living in the United States. Here are some key financial benchmarks from that time:

Average Cost of a New House: Owning a new house in 1964 came at an average cost of approximately $13,050. This price point reflected the affordability of homeownership during that period.

Average Income per Year: The average annual income for individuals in 1964 was around $6,000. This income level provided the financial foundation for many households.

Average Monthly Rent: For those who opted for renting, the average monthly rent was approximately $115. This figure represented the cost of housing for those who preferred not to buy a home.

Average Monthly Rent: For those who opted for renting, the average monthly rent was approximately $115. This figure represented the cost of housing for those who preferred not to buy a home.

Loaf of Bread: A basic staple like a loaf of bread cost around 21 cents. This affordable price made it feasible for households to include bread in their daily meals.

United States Postage Stamp: Sending mail was cost-effective, with a postage stamp priced at 5 cents. This made staying connected through letters and correspondence affordable.

Ticket to the Movies: Enjoying a night at the movies came at a relatively low cost, with a movie ticket priced at $1.25. This made cinematic entertainment an accessible pastime for many.

THE BEATLES Concert Ticket 1964

These cost-of-living figures from 1964 reflect a time when affordability and accessibility were key aspects of American life. It's a glimpse into the financial landscape of that era, where everyday expenses allowed individuals and families to enjoy various aspects of life without breaking the bank.

Activity
1964 Shopping List Challenge

Instructions:

• Below, you'll find a list of common household items and groceries that were available in 1964. We've included the approximate prices these items would have cost during that time.

• Your task is to create your own shopping list by selecting items from the provided list. Imagine you're shopping in 1964, and choose the items you would need for your daily life.

• Next to each selected item, write down the 1964 price. You can use the provided prices as a reference or conduct your own research to estimate the costs.

• Calculate the total cost of your shopping list based on the 1964 prices. Take a moment to compare this cost with today's prices for the same items, if you wish.

• Share your reflections on the activity. What surprised you the most about the cost differences between 1964 and today? How do you think these changes have affected people's lives?

• Gallon of milk: $1.061
• A loaf of bread averaged 22¢
• Coffee was 79¢ a pound
• A gallon of milk averaged $1.08
• A telephone call from a pay phone was 10¢
• A 26" color TV averaged $379
• Minimum wage was $1.15
• Beatles albums had the list price of $5.98

SHOPPING *List*

	Item	Price	# Units	Total Price
☐				
☐				
☐				
☐				
☐				
☐				
☐				
☐				
☐				
☐				
☐				
☐				
☐				
☐				
☐				
☐				
☐				
☐				
☐				
☐				
			Total	

Chapter 8:
Iconic Advertisements of 1964

8.1 Remembering Vintage Ads

1964 Pepsi Cola Vintage Advertisement: This ad showcases the timeless appeal of Pepsi Cola. Can you recognize the distinctive logo that has graced Pepsi products for decades?

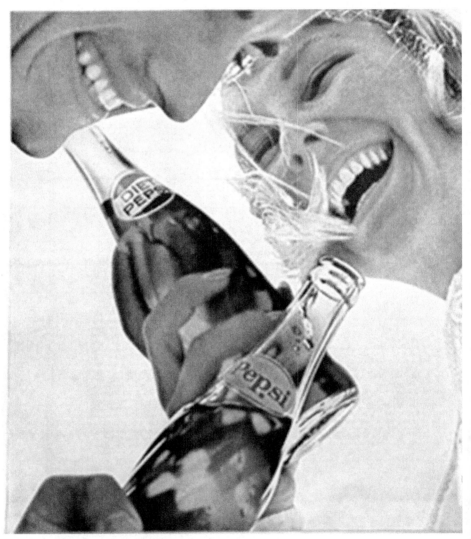

1964 Pepsi Cola Vintage Advertisement

1964 Coke Advertisement: Coca-Cola, the world's favorite soda, has a logo that's instantly recognizable. See if you can spot it in this vintage Coke ad.

1964 Coke Advertisement

Vintage 1964 Bell Telephone Advertisement by Robert Kinser: Bell Telephone was a communication giant in 1964. Try to identify their logo in this nostalgic ad.

Vintage 1964 Bell Telephone Advertisement by Robert Kinser

1964 Colgate Toothpaste Vintage Ad: Colgate has been a trusted name in oral care for generations. Can you find their logo in this classic toothpaste ad?

Do
something
about
cavities now

Get
Colgate –
THE
BIG
ONE!

1964 Colgate Toothpaste Vintage Ad

1964 Kool-Aid Drink Mix Beverage: Kool-Aid was a popular beverage choice in 1964. See if you can spot the logo that represents this fruity drink mix.

1964 Kool-Aid Drink Mix Beverage

1964 Vintage ad for Budweiser Beer: Budweiser, the king of beers, had a distinctive logo even in 1964. Try to identify it in this vintage beer ad.

1964 Vintage ad for Budweiser Beer

1964 Viceroy Cigarettes: Viceroy cigarettes were known for their unique flavor. Look closely to see if you can recognize the Viceroy logo in this old cigarette ad.

1964 Viceroy Cigarettes

Activity:
Brand Logo Challenge
Identify the Brands from '64

Step into the past with these vintage advertisements from 1964 and put your brand recognition skills to the test. Challenge yourself and your friends to identify the brands based on their iconic logos from that era. It's a fun and nostalgic journey down memory lane. Let the challenge begin!

Instructions:

• Examine each vintage advertisement carefully.

• Try to identify the brand associated with the provided logo.

• Write down your guesses for each advertisement.

• Compare your answers with your friends and see who can score the highest!

Let the nostalgia-filled Brand Logo Challenge begin!

1. Your guessing:..

Who made the
orange more tempting
than the apple?

2. Your guessing:..

3. Your guessing:..

THE LUXURY SIX FOR THE MAN WHO WANTS SOMETHING BETTER!

4. Your guessing:..

Embracing 1964: A Grateful Farewell

Thank you for joining us on this journey through a year that holds a special place in our hearts. Whether you experienced 1964 firsthand or through the pages of this book, we hope it brought you moments of joy, nostalgia, and connection to a time that will forever shine brightly in our memories.

Share Your Thoughts and Help Us Preserve History

Your support and enthusiasm for this journey mean the world to us. We invite you to share your thoughts, leave a review, and keep the spirit of '64 alive. As we conclude our adventure, we look forward to more journeys through the annals of history together. Until then, farewell and thank you for the memories.

We would like to invite you to explore more of our fantastic world by scanning the QR code below. There you can easily get free ebooks from us and receive so many surprises.

Happy Birthday

note

TO DO LIST

- ○ --
- ○ --
- ○ --
- ○ --
- ○ --
- ○ --
- ○ --
- ○ --
- ○ --
- ○ --
- ○ --
- ○ --
- ○ --
- ○ --

well
done!

To Do List

TO DO LIST

Name: _____   Day: _____   Month: _____

No	To Do List	Yes	No

TO DO LIST

Name: _____   Day: _____   Month: _____

No	To Do List	Yes	No

TO DO LIST

Name: _____   Day: _____   Month: _____

No	To Do List	Yes	No

NOTE

NOTE

POSTCARD

To:

From:

Remember This!

WISH YOU WERE HERE,
123 ANYWHERE ST., ANY CITY

To Do List

- [ ] _____
- [ ] _____
- [ ] _____
- [ ] _____
- [ ] _____
- [ ] _____
- [ ] _____
- [ ] _____
- [ ] _____
- [ ] _____
- [ ] _____
- [ ] _____
- [ ] _____
- [ ] _____

HAPPY BIRTHDAY NOTE